Malachi: Finding Hope in the Midst of Adversity

Dr. Terry W. Dorsett

Malachi: Finding Hope in the Midst of Adversity

Copyright © 2012 by Dr. Terry W. Dorsett. All rights reserved.

1st Edition (Rev.04c): April, 2012

ISBN: 978-1-105-66008-5

Unless otherwise noted, all Scripture quotations are taken from the Holman Christian Standard Bible®, Copyright © 1999, 2000, 2002, 2003, 2009 by Holman Bible Publishers. Used by permission. Holman Christian Standard Bible®, Holman CSB® and HCSB® are federally registered trademarks of Holman Bible Publishers.

Additional copies of this book may be purchased online at: http://www.lulu.com/spotlight/DrTerryWDorsett.

Contact: www.terrydorsett.com
Write to: Next Generation Evangelistic Network
30 Jones Brothers Way, Suite B
Barre, VT 05641

E-Publisher: Lulu Enterprises, Inc., lulu.com
3101 Hillsborough Street
Raleigh, NC 27607

RELIGION / Christian Education / Adult
Small-group Bible study about Malachi
Paperback: 6.00 x 9.00 x 0.20 in (84 pp.)

Cover photo and photos, pages 7, 17, 29, 39, 49, 59, and 67 by Kay Dorsett. Instructional design, book formatting, and assembly services provided by Darryl Ann and Wayne Lavitt (visit christians-coffee-breaks.com).

CONTENTS

Malachi: Finding Hope in the Midst of Adversity.....1

Introduction..5
Lesson 1: Tough Love..7
Lesson 2: A Covenant of Life and Peace............................17
Lesson 3: Have We Wearied the Lord?...............................29
Lesson 4: Refiner's Fire...39
Lesson 5: The Importance of Tithing..................................49
Lesson 6: The Law of Sowing and Reaping......................59
Lesson 7: Judgment Day..67
Outline for Malachi..77
About the Author..81
Finding Real Hope...83

Acknowledgment

I would like to thank my wife, Kay Dorsett, for providing the photographs that grace these pages of my study on Malachi. She captured the key moments of our 2011 trip to Israel and selected appropriate photos to go with each lesson.

Previous Works by Dr. Terry W. Dorsett

- *Developing Leadership Teams in the Bivocational Church* (Bloomington, IN: CrossBooks, 2010).
- *Bible Brain Teasers: Fun Adventures Through the Bible* (Raleigh, NC: Lulu Enterprises, Inc., 2011).
- *Creating Effective Partnerships - Strategies for Increasing Kingdom Impact* (Raleigh, NC: Lulu Enterprises, Inc., 2012).
- *Mission Possible: Reaching the Next Generation through the Small Church* (Bloomington, IN: CrossBooks, 2012).

Information for ordering Dr. Dorsett's books is found on page 82.

Introduction

Few Christians study the book of Malachi. Of those who do, many view it in a negative light because the book addresses the subject of judgment in a number of passages. But Malachi is not just about judgment. It also contains a message of hope. Malachi urged the Jews to find hope in the midst of the adversity they were facing in their lives.

Malachi also contains a message of love. God was warning the people one last time before judgment fell. Even though the people had already been warned many times and had numerous chances to turn from their sinful ways, God loved them so much that He wanted to give them one last opportunity to make things right.

After Malachi's ministry ended, a period of 400 years followed in which there was no prophet in Israel who spoke for God. That was a long time without a clear word from the Lord. During that time many bad things happened to the nation. The nation could have been spared many of those things had they heeded Malachi's message of hope in the midst of adversity.

As we consider the modern world in which we live, with all our efforts to remove God from public life and discard our Christian heritage, we might want to pay attention to the warnings God gives us in this ancient book. We should study Malachi with a heart of love instead of a heart of defensiveness. God is trying one more time to reach us before it is too late. Will we listen?

Dr. Terry W. Dorsett
Spring, 2012

NOTE: Since presenting my study of Malachi as a sermon series and posting it on my blog (terrydorsett.com), I have received a number of thoughtful comments and testimonies from fellow Christians. I have included some of these at the end of each lesson in the "We Are Listening!" section. Keep sending those emails and blog postings. I may include your comments in a future edition!

Lesson 1: Tough Love

1.1 Scripture: Malachi 1:1-3, 6-9, 14

¹ An oracle: The word of the LORD to Israel through Malachi. ² "I have loved you," says the LORD. But you ask: "How have You loved us?" "Wasn't Esau Jacob's brother?" This is the LORD's declaration. "Even so, I loved Jacob, ³ but I hated Esau. I turned his mountains into a wasteland, and gave his inheritance to the desert jackals." ⁶ "A son honors his father and a servant his master. But if I am a father, where is My honor? And if I am a master, where is your fear of Me? says the LORD of Hosts to you priests, who despise My name." Yet you ask: "How have we despised Your name?" ⁷ "By presenting defiled food on My altar." You ask: "How have we defiled You?" When you say: "The LORD's table is contemptible." ⁸ "When you present a blind animal for sacrifice, is it not wrong? And when you present a lame or sick animal, is it not wrong? Bring it to your governor! Would he be pleased with you or show you favor?" asks the LORD of Hosts. ⁹ "And now ask for God's favor. Will He be gracious to us? Since this has come from your hands, will He show any of you favor?" asks the LORD of Hosts. [14] *"The deceiver is cursed who has an acceptable male in his flock and makes a vow but sacrifices a defective animal to the Lord. For I am a great King," says the LORD of Hosts, "and My name will be feared among the nations."*

1.2 Lesson Points

- 1.3.1. God speaks to man.
- 1.3.2. God loves man.
- 1.3.3. God deserves honor.
- 1.3.4. God deserves our sacrifice.
- 1.3.5. God deserves our best.
- 1.3.6. Do we receive much and give little?
- 1.3.7. God is King among nations.

1.3 Today's Lesson

1.3.1. God speaks to man.

Verse 1 - An oracle: The word of the LORD to Israel through Malachi.

- Malachi was the last prophet in the Old Testament. When Malachi finished his ministry, the Lord did not speak through another prophet for 400 years.
- Very little is known about the man Malachi. He might have been a priest. What is known is that he lived in a time in which people had begun to fall away from their faith.
- The word *oracle* is from the Hebrew word *masa* and literally means *a burden*.

- Malachi was burdened by what he saw in his society and felt compelled to try to help people see the error of their ways.
- Though sometimes prophets are seen as being judgmental, they are actually motivated by a deep burden over the pain they see in the lives of those who chose a lifestyle of sin.
- What sins do we observe in our culture that burden us?

    _____
    _____
    _____
    _____
    _____

- What have we done to address those burdens?

    _____
    _____
    _____
    _____
    _____

1.3.2. God loves man.

Verse 2 - I have loved you, says the LORD. But you ask: How have You loved us? Wasn't Esau Jacob's brother? This is the LORD's declaration. Even so, I loved Jacob, but I hated Esau.

- The message that God told Malachi to give to Israel was one of love.
- Although Malachi was going to be showing "tough love," it really was God's love that Malachi was trying to convey.
- Most of us do not like tough love. But real love compels us to do what it takes to actually help others, not just what makes them (or us) feel good for the moment.

- List one example of tough love we have had to show someone else:

  _____
  _____
  _____
  _____

- The Israelites were struggling to hear God's message of love because of the difficulties in their lives, so they asked Malachi how God had demonstrated His love for them.
- When we go through a hard time in our own lives, it is easy to begin to feel like God no longer loves us.
- It is easy to focus on the negative things in life and forget all that God is doing.
- What are some difficult experiences we are having right now in our lives?

  _____
  _____
  _____
  _____

- What are positive things God might be doing through the difficulties we listed above?

  _____
  _____
  _____
  _____

- Malachi used a unique illustration to point out to the Israelites how God had loved them.
- Malachi said that God loved "Jacob" but hated "Esau."

- To understand this illustration we must know a little about history. The Jews descended from Jacob and though they were having a hard time, they had been able to return to their land and rebuild their temple and have a somewhat normal life. This was a demonstration of God's love for them, even in the midst of their struggles.
- The Arabs descended from Esau and at that point in history had been utterly decimated as a people. They had not yet been able to rebuild their nation. It lay in ruins no matter what they had tried to do.
- Were the Jews better than the Arabs?
- Did the Jews deserve to be blessed more than the Arabs?
- No. Both groups had done wrong and both groups had received the punishment they had deserved.
- But God, in His mercy and grace, had chosen to help the Jews rebuild their nation.
- God demonstrated His love to them in this way.
- Life may not have been perfect for the Jews, but it was far better than many of the people around them.
- We have all done many stupid things in our lives.
- We have all received "rewards" for our mistakes and carry certain burdens as a result of past actions.
- But sometimes God chooses to bless us in spite of ourselves as a demonstration of His love.
- List some blessings God has given to us in spite of some mistakes we have made:

  _____
  _____
  _____
  _____
  _____

- We should never doubt the love of God in our lives, even when things are not going well.

- We do not have to look far to find someone in far worse shape than we are.
- Whatever we have, as little as it may seem at the moment, is a gift of love from God.

1.3.3. God deserves honor.

Verse 6 - A son honors his father and a servant his master. But if I am a father, where is My honor? And if I am a master, where is your fear of Me?

- As believers "we are God's children" (Romans 8:16).
- Read John 1:12 and write the main thought of that verse below:

_____
_____
_____
_____
_____

- Children are supposed to honor their parents.
- Read Ephesians 6:1-2 and write the main thought of those verses below:

_____
_____
_____
_____
_____

- Unfortunately, the Israelites had forgotten to honor God as their Heavenly Father.
- List one example of a time we forget to honor God?

_____
_____
_____
_____
_____

What was the result?

_____
_____
_____
_____

- God calls Christians to reorder our priorities and to follow Him.
- Read Luke 9:23 and write the main thought below:

_____
_____
_____
_____

- The Israelites had left God off their priority list and were following their own ways instead of God's ways.
- Do we ever follow our own way instead of God's way? Do our priorities ever get messed up?

1.3.4. God deserves our sacrifice.

Verse 8 - When you present a blind animal for sacrifice, is it not wrong? And when you present a lame or sick animal, is it not wrong? Bring it to your governor! Would he be pleased with you or show you favor?

- The Jews protested Malachi's strong words.
- They did not see their failure to love God nor did they see their failure to follow God's ways.
- Malachi points out just one example of how they had failed to love God the way they should have.
- The Old Testament had very strict guidelines about what the people could bring to sacrifice when they worshipped the Lord.

- They were supposed to bring a healthy lamb or goat that was at least a year old and looked perfect.
- The whole point was that it was supposed to cost them something. After all, a sacrifice was not supposed to be free.
- Instead of doing that, they had been bringing sick animals that they could do nothing else with anyway and giving that as a sacrifice to the Lord. This was really not a sacrifice at all.
- Malachi points out that if they had tried to pay their taxes with such a sickly animal, the governor would have rejected it. Yet they thought such a sickly animal would be good enough for God.
- We often think we can give God our leftovers and that it will please Him.
- List some examples of how people in our modern times try to give God leftovers:

_____
_____
_____
_____
_____

- We should be offering God our best because we love Him and we want to serve Him.
- If we gave our spouse or our best friend the kind of love we give God, how long would that relationship last? If someone offered that kind of love to us, how would it make us feel?

1.3.5. God deserves our best.

Verse 14a - The deceiver is cursed who has an acceptable male in his flock and makes a vow but sacrifices a defective animal to the Lord.

- God was not trying to be mean and demand more than the people could give.

- God would not have been upset if they had given their best even if their best was not as nice as someone else's.
- God was sad because clearly they could have done better but they tried to deceive God.
- God knows our hearts and sees through all our motivations.
- God knows when we have given our best and when we have given just enough to try to look good in front of others.

1.3.6. Do we receive much and give little?

Verse 9 - "And now ask for God's favor. Will He be gracious to us? Since this has come from your hands, will He show any of you favor?" asks the LORD of Hosts.

- Malachi was trying to help the Jews understand that if they did their least for God, then they should not expect God to bless them.
- God does often bless us in spite of our behavior, but we should not think we "deserve" those blessings.
- Too many people think of God as a cosmic ATM machine. They want a "spiritual drive-through" from which they can make withdrawals any given time.
- That is not how spirituality works. But even if it did work that way, why would we think we could withdraw something from an account that was already empty!

1.3.7. God is King among nations.

Verse 14b - ... For I am a great King, says the LORD of Hosts, and My name will be feared among the nations.

- Malachi explains that the Lord is a great King.

- The Lord's people are supposed to be a great people.
- If God's people do not act great, it makes God look bad.
- Sometimes God has to give His people tough love so that they can get back in line and live right. But it is still love.

1.4 What Have We Learned?

- God always loves us, even when we are going through difficult times.
- God expects us to give Him our best. God knows our inner motivations and whether our effort really is our best or not.
- We cannot live in ways that do not honor the Lord and still expect God's blessings on our lives.
- We must live in a way that proclaims God's greatness to those around us.

1.5 We Are Listening!

Some of the responses we have received to this lesson include:

- "The part about the Israelites bringing sickly 'leftover' animals as a sacrifice made me re-evaluate my schedule and budget. Am I giving Him leftovers?" —*Wayne, S. Burlington, VT*
- "I have been studying this book the last few months. Thank you for helping me understand it better!" —*Kathleen, Barre, VT*

Lesson 2: A Covenant of Life and Peace

2.1 Scripture: Malachi 2:1-9

¹ "Therefore, this decree is for you priests: ² If you don't listen, and if you don't take it to heart to honor My name," says the LORD of Hosts, "I will send a curse among you, and I will curse your blessings. In fact, I have already begun to curse them because you are not taking it to heart. ³ "Look, I am going to rebuke your descendants, and I will spread animal waste over your faces, the waste from your festival sacrifices, and you will be taken away with it. ⁴ Then you will know that I sent you this decree so My covenant with Levi may continue," says the LORD of Hosts. ⁵ "My covenant with him was one of life and peace, and I gave these to him; it called for reverence, and he revered Me and stood in awe of My name. ⁶ True instruction was in his mouth, and nothing wrong was found on his lips. He walked with Me in peace and fairness and turned many from sin. ⁷ For the lips of a priest should guard knowledge, and people should seek instruction from his mouth, because he is the messenger of the LORD of Hosts. [8] *"You, on the other hand, have turned from the way. You have caused many to stumble by your instruction. You have violated the covenant of Levi," says the LORD of Hosts.* [9] *"So I in turn have made you despised and humiliated before all the people because you are not keeping My ways but are showing partiality in your instruction."*

2.2 Lesson Points

- 2.3.1. Christian leaders should set an example.
- 2.3.2. Christians should be an example to society.
- 2.3.3. Christians should not be a curse to others.
- 2.3.4. Christian parents are an example to their children.
- 2.3.5. God promises life and peace.
- 2.3.6. Spiritual leaders must speak the truth.
- 2.3.7. Spiritual leaders guard the knowledge of God.
- 2.3.8. Christians should not be the cause of others turning away from God.
- 2.3.9. The shame of sin should lead to repentance.

2.3 Today's Lesson

2.3.1. Spiritual leaders should set an example.

Verse 1 - Therefore, this decree is for you priests.

- In the Old Testament, people did not go to God directly. They went through a priest.
- The priests were supposed to be holy and set a right example for people to follow.
- Unfortunately, priests often failed to set the example they should.

- Malachi had a strong word of rebuke for those corrupt priests.
- In the New Testament we learn that all Christian believers are priests before God.
- Read Hebrews 10:19 and summarize it below:

_____
_____
_____
_____

- Read Ephesians 2:18 and summarize it below:

_____
_____
_____
_____

- Read 1 Timothy 2:5 and summarize it below:

_____
_____
_____
_____

- Read 1 Peter 2:4 and summarize it below:

_____
_____
_____
_____

- Read Romans 12:1 and summarize it below:

_____
_____
_____
_____

- Christians no longer have to go through a human priest to get to God. Through faith in Christ we gain direct access to God the Father.
- This means that in our modern times each Christian holds the responsibility of being a priest. We often refer to this as the "priesthood of the believer." As priests, all Christians must live right so that non-Christians can see Christ in our lives.

2.3.2. Christians should be an example to society.

Verse 2 - "If you don't listen, and if you don't take it to heart to honor My name," says the LORD of Hosts, "I will send a curse among you, and I will curse your blessings."

- In the Old Testament, if the priests did not listen to what God was saying and take God's Word to heart, they would be cursed.
- The blessings they were supposed to give to others would become curses instead.
- Since all Christian believers are now priests before God, that means that we must listen to what God says and take it to heart.
- If we fail to do so, the blessing we are supposed to be in society will become a curse instead.
- List ways in which we have been a blessing to our community:

_____
_____
_____
_____
_____

2.3.3. Christians should not be a curse to others.

Verse 2 - . . . In fact, I have already begun to curse them because you are not taking it to heart.

- Malachi goes on to say that the conversion of blessings into curses had already begun to happen. It was not yet full blown, but the process had started.
- We have also started to see this happening in our own society.
- As the church has lost its vision and forgotten its purpose, people have begun to despise the church.
- For the last few years we have seen our society push the church farther and farther away from the public view.
- This will continue until the church once again becomes a blessing to our society.

2.3.4. Christian parents are an example to their children.

Verse 3 - I am going to rebuke your descendants, and I will spread animal waste over your faces, the waste from your festival sacrifices, and you will be taken away with it.

- God said that not only would the priests themselves be cursed, but their descendants would also pay a price.
- Descendants mean more than just our immediate children. This also applies to future generations.
- List one action that our grandparents took that continues to impact our lives:

    _____
    _____
    _____
    _____

- List one action that we are taking now that may impact our grandchildren in the future:

  _____
  _____
  _____
  _____

- Children learn by our bad examples and then repeat our mistakes, which are then repeated by the next generation.
- This cycle of pain will continue until someone determines to break the cycle and start living as God intended us to live.
- But there is also a spiritual element to all of this, what some theologians refer to as a "generational curse."
- Though the concept of generational curses can be confusing, the basic premise is that if we let a negative spiritual force enter into our lives, that spiritual force will cling to us and continue to cause spiritual pain until we cast it off in the name of Christ.
- Read Exodus 20:5 and 34:7 and summarize these verses below:

  _____
  _____
  _____
  _____
  _____

- Read Numbers 14:18 and summarize it below:

  _____
  _____
  _____
  _____
  _____

- Read Deuteronomy 5:9 and summarize it below:

_____
_____
_____
_____
_____

- Those negative spiritual forces—which may also be referred to as demons—enjoy being attached to humans, and they love to invade whole families and keep them in spiritual bondage.
- They jump from generation to generation in joyful glee at keeping families enslaved.
- When a generational curse attaches itself to our family, we often feel so bad about ourselves and our families that it seems as if we have animal dung smeared all over us (as Malachi said in verse 3).
- We feel useless and like a pile of trash that needs to be hauled away.
- The devil loves it when Christians feel like trash!
- If we are feeling like trash then we will be emotionally and spiritually paralyzed and be ineffective in our Christian walk with God.
- The good news is that Christ did not come so we would continue to feel like trash. He came to set us free of generational curses and give us abundant life!
- It is important to understand that though Christians cannot be demon possessed, they can be demon oppressed. Being oppressed is a terrible experience.
- A word of caution: We should not think that every time we have a bad day we are being oppressed by a demon.
- The devil is not THAT strong. Sometimes, we are just having a bad day.
- To know if negative experiences are really spiritual warfare we must first eliminate all the "normal" things that might cause negative experiences. For

example, if we lost our driver's license because we were driving under the influence of alcohol, the loss of our license is not a demonic attack. It is the normal result of our sin. If we stop driving drunk, the issue of losing our license will go away naturally.
- Once we have eliminated all the normal possibilities, if the negative experiences and feelings of bondage continue, then we may conclude that it is a spiritual attack.
- Christians need to claim the freedom they have been given from generational curses.
- We may need to find a spiritual mentor to help us deal with the behavioral issues we are struggling to overcome.
- Read Galatians 3:13 and summarize it below:

_____
_____
_____
_____
_____

- Read James 4:7 and summarize it below:

_____
_____
_____
_____
_____

- Read 1 John 1:9 and summarize it below:

_____
_____
_____
_____
_____

2.3.5. God promises life and peace.

Verse 5 - "My covenant with him was one of life and peace, and I gave these to him; it called for reverence, and he revered Me and stood in awe of My name."

- God reminded the Old Testament priests that His original covenant with them was one of life and peace.
- Life means being connected to God and to other people in a healthy wonderful way.
- Peace means having a calm, happy life filled with purpose and meaning.
- God made this covenant of life and peace with the Old Testament priests, but to keep it they had to honor God and follow Him.
- When they failed to do that, they lost the benefits of the covenant.
- The same thing has happened to Christians today.
- Through Christ, God the Father has made a covenant of life and peace with us.
- To receive the benefits of the covenant, we must honor God and follow Him.
- When we fail to do that, we do not receive the benefits of our faith.
- We must remember that there is no benefit without responsibility.

2.3.6. Spiritual leaders must speak the truth.

Verse 6 - True instruction was in his mouth, and nothing wrong was found on his lips. He walked with Me in peace and fairness and turned many from sin.

- The priest who honored the covenant spoke the truth and did not say things that were wrong.
- The priest who honored the covenant treated people fairly.

- The priest who honored the covenant turned many people away from sin.
- This is the kind of priest we should desire to be.

2.3.7. Spiritual leaders guard the knowledge of God.

Verse 7 - For the lips of a priest should guard knowledge, and people should seek instruction from his mouth, because he is the messenger of the LORD of Hosts.

- The priest who honored the covenant guarded the knowledge of God so that it did not get watered down through the generations.
- How we are guarding the knowledge of God and passing it to our children or grandchildren?

_____
_____
_____
_____

- People came to good priests to ask for spiritual instructions.
- When was the last time someone asked us for spiritual guidance and what did they ask?

_____
_____
_____
_____
_____

2.3.8. Christians should not be the cause of others turning away from God.

Verse 8 - You, on the other hand, have turned from the way. You have caused many to stumble by your instruction. You have violated the covenant . . .

- God rebuked the Old Testament priests harshly because they had done the exact opposite of what they were supposed to be doing.
- Since we are all now priests before God, we should be careful not to cause people to stumble.
- List some behaviors in our lives that may cause others to stumble and what we can do to begin to change those behaviors:

_____

_____

_____

_____

_____

2.3.9. The shame of sin should lead to repentance.

Verse 9 - So I in turn have made you despised and humiliated before all the people because you are not keeping My ways . . .

- The punishment for not keeping the covenant of life and peace was to be despised and humiliated before others.
- If we are not really living the way a Christian should live, it can be a terrible thing when people begin to find out what we are really like.
- Are we happy with what we have become?
- Do we need to repent of some behavior and return to God?

2.4 What Have We Learned?

- We should recognize that God wants us to accept a covenant of life and peace with Him.
- To receive the benefits of that covenant we must honor God and live as He wants us to.

- When we fail to do that, our blessings become curses instead.
- We can pass those curses on to our families if we do not repent of them.
- When we repent of our sins and determine to break the cycle of sin that grips our families, we can renew the covenant of life and peace that God has between us and Him.

2.5 We Are Listening!

Some of the responses we have received to this lesson include:

- "Malachi was so graphic, using 'animal waste' to make a point about parents setting a bad example for their children. My Christian dad said that in our early family years, he had a hard time quitting the smoking habit. One day, as a boy, I pulled a pack from his pocket, and asked if I could have one. He quit smoking that very day! That had a permanent impression on me. I never had a smoke, and never had to deal with that habit. I praise God my dad worked to set a godly example." —*Anonymous, Burlington, Vermont*
- "This really made me think. I want to set a godly example for my kids. I have not always done that. I am working to change that." —*Al, McCory, Arkansas*

Lesson 3: Have We Wearied the Lord?

3.1 Scripture: Malachi 2:10-17

^{10} Don't all of us have one Father? Didn't one God create us? Why then do we act treacherously against one another, profaning the covenant of our fathers? ^{11} Judah has acted treacherously, and a detestable thing has been done in Israel and in Jerusalem. For Judah has profaned the LORD's sanctuary, which He loves, and has married the daughter of a foreign god. ^{12} To the man who does this, may the LORD cut off any descendants from the tents of Jacob, even if they present an offering to the LORD of Hosts. ^{13} And this is another thing you do: you cover the LORD's altar with tears, with weeping and groaning, because He no longer respects your offerings or receives them gladly from your hands. ^{14} Yet you ask, "For what reason?" Because the LORD has been a witness between you and the wife of your youth. You have acted treacherously against her, though she was your marriage partner and your wife by covenant. ^{15} Didn't the one God make us with a remnant

of His life-breath? And what does the One seek? A godly offspring. So watch yourselves carefully, and do not act treacherously against the wife of your youth. ^{16} *"If he hates and divorces his wife," says the LORD God of Israel, "he covers his garment with injustice," says the LORD of Hosts. Therefore, watch yourselves carefully, and do not act treacherously.* ^{17} *You have wearied the LORD with your words. Yet you ask, "How have we wearied Him?" When you say, "Everyone who does evil is good in the LORD's sight, and He is pleased with them," or "Where is the God of justice?"*

3.2 Lesson Points

- 3.3.1. Christians should not deal treacherously with each other.
- 3.3.2. Christians should only marry fellow believers.
- 3.3.3. Christians should turn away from sin.
- 3.3.4. Christians should not lust after another spouse.
- 3.3.5. Christians should produce spiritual fruit.
- 3.3.6. Christians should not weary God with insincerity.

3.3 Today's Lesson

3.3.1. Christians should not deal treacherously with each other.

Verse 10 - Don't all of us have one Father? Didn't one God create us? Why then do we act treacherously against one another . . .

- The prophet Malachi boldly confronted the bad behaviors that were prevalent in his society.
- One of those bad behaviors was that people treated each other treacherously.

- The Hebrew word for *treacherous* is *begad*, which refers to deceiving someone on purpose.
- The Israelites were purposely deceiving each other in a variety of ways and it was destroying the fabric of their society.
- Malachi reminded the people that each person was created in the image of God.
- That means that all people deserve to be treated with respect because the image of God is stamped on each person's soul.
- We do not have to agree with all the choices other people make, but we do have to treat other people with respect because they are created in the image of God.
- That image may be marred by sin, but it is still the image of God and that should mean something to those who follow God.

3.3.2. Christians should only marry fellow believers.

Verse 11 - . . . Judah has profaned the LORD's sanctuary, which He loves, and has married the daughter of a foreign god.

- The Hebrew word for *profane* is *chalal*. It refers to polluting something so badly that it no longer has value.
- This verse has both a literal and figurative interpretation.
- The men of Judah had literally married women who worshiped foreign gods. This was strictly forbidden by God in the Old Testament.
- Marrying women who worshipped foreign gods was not an issue of ethnicity. Malachi had just made the point that we are all created by God in His image and therefore all people are equal regardless of their ethnicity.

- The problem was that these ladies did not follow the true God of Heaven, but worshipped false idols.
- The people of Judah had been swayed by the false religions that these marriages had exposed them too. Their faith in the true God had begun to waver as a result.
- This ancient verse still applies to Christians in our modern time. Christians should only marry people who share our Christian faith.
- Read 2 Corinthians 6:14 and summarize its teachings below:

_____
_____
_____
_____
_____

- While there are some marriages in which a non-Christian spouse will decide that they want to become Christian, it does not happen often.
- This puts tremendous pressure on a marriage because faith binds our hearts together. If we do not share the same faith, then we will be missing a key element in the bonding process.
- If we are unmarried, we should only date Christians.
- If we are already in a mixed-faith marriage, we should earnestly pray that God will allow us to be one of those rare marriages where the non-believing partner will choose to believe.
- We can also apply this same concept to any area of life, not just marriage.
- Though it is fine to have non-Christian friends, we should be careful how they affect us.
- When we allow non-Christian ideas and concepts to begin to influence us more than our faith, then we have figuratively married a foreign god and it can only bring pain and hurt into our lives.

- The most miserable person in the world is the Christian who knows they are not living the way God wants them to live.

3.3.3. Christians should turn away from sin.

Verse 13 - And this is another thing you do: you cover the LORD's altar with tears, with weeping and groaning, because He no longer respects your offerings or receives them gladly from your hands.

- Malachi also confronts the peoples' attempts to manipulate God through false piety.
- They would come to the altar and weep and groan over their problems, but they were not willing to actually change their bad behavior.
- Acting sad is not the same thing as repenting of our sin.
- Repentance is turning away from sin and turning toward God.
- When we really repent, we can expect God's blessings on our lives.
- When we are just sad that we got caught, we should not be looking for a blessing.
- God no longer received their offerings or prayers because they wanted the benefits of faith without the responsibilities of repentance that came with it.
- If our prayers do not seem to be working, we should examine our level of repentance to ensure it is genuine.

3.3.4. Christians should not lust after another spouse.

Verse 14 - Yet you ask, "For what reason?" Because the LORD has been a witness between you and the wife of your youth. You have acted treacherously against her …

- Though there were many areas of the Israelites' lives that did not please God, the one that most upset God was the way the men were treating their wives.
- In that time period, Jewish culture was extremely male dominated.
- Women were completely dependent on men for their livelihood.
- When a man married a woman, he made a life-long commitment to provide for her.
- He if broke that commitment, the woman was in a very difficult situation because she had no other means of support.
- In Malachi's day, men had made commitments to their wives when they were young, but as the women had gotten older, the men desired other women, presumably ones that were younger and prettier.
- God said He would not honor the prayers of men who treated their wives this way.
- In our modern world, men and women are often considered equals.
- In our modern world, both men and women are guilty of lusting after someone to whom they are not married. That lust often leads to sinful behavior.
- Christians cannot expect to be blessed by God if we allow lust to control us in this way.

3.3.5. Christians should produce spiritual fruit.

Verse 15 - Didn't the one God make us with a remnant of His life-breath? And what does the One seek? A godly offspring.

- Not only are we created in the image of God, but God breathed into us the breath of life.

- Read Genesis 2:7 and write a summary of it below:

  _____
  _____
  _____
  _____

- God's breath is more than just oxygen. It refers to His spiritual nature which He breathed into humankind at creation.
- The primary difference between humans and animals is that humankind has a spiritual nature.
- What does God's spiritual nature produce?

  _____
  _____
  _____
  _____

- People also have a spiritual nature.
- What should our own spiritual nature produce?

  _____
  _____
  _____
  _____

- One "offspring" of our own spiritual nature should be other people who share our spiritual values. We should be sharing our faith and helping others embrace it.
- When we fail to produce spiritual fruit in our lives, we fail in the very essence of our faith.

3.3.6. Christians should not weary God with insincerity.

Verse 17 - You have wearied the LORD with your words. Yet you ask, "How have we wearied Him?"

When you say, "Everyone who does evil is good in the LORD's sight, and He is pleased with them," or "Where is the God of justice?"

- God had grown weary of their bad behavior.
- Ever ready with an excuse, the people asked how they had wearied God.
- Malachi tells his audience that they had wearied the Lord with all their talk which was not backed up by action.
- Malachi then pointed out two specific things that wearied God:
    - First, they claimed that people who were doing evil were actually good.
    - Second, they accused God of not being just.
- Make a list of bad things that our own society often calls good:

    _____
    _____
    _____
    _____

- Take a moment and reflect on whether current events might indicate that God has grown tired of our culture calling this list of bad things good.
- Our society also often accuses God of not being just when He does not do things the way we wish He would.
- Make a list of things that happen for which people like to blame God:

    _____
    _____
    _____
    _____

- If we were God, how would we respond to someone calling us unjust when we had done all the right things?

  _____
  _____
  _____
  _____
  _____

- We should be thankful that God has great patience.
- We should be thankful that God has shown us love that we do not deserve.
- We should be thankful that God has withheld judgment that we do deserve.
- But we should never forget that at some point, God will decide that enough is enough.
- When God decides that we have wearied Him enough, the Day of Judgment will come!
- When the Day of Judgment finally happens, we had better be on God's side and not still playing spiritual games.
- None of us know when that day will be, but it is much closer for us than it was for Malachi.

3.4 What Have We Learned?

- If we are purposefully deceitful of others, we should not expect God to bless us.
- We should be careful not to let anything draw us away from God, even our marriages.
- When we realize we have done wrong, we must repent of that behavior and change it.
- If we are living right before God, we should be producing spiritual fruit in our own lives and in the lives of others.

- Though we should be thankful for God's patience, grace and mercy, we should not use them as an excuse to continue wrong behavior.

3.5 We Are Listening!

Some of the responses we have received to this lesson include:

- "Thank you, Dr. Dorsett, for this study of Malachi. His words are so relevant for what we face today. God's words are timeless." —*Wayne, S. Burlington, Vermont*
- "I really liked this lesson. We usually prefer warm and fuzzy sermons. This one makes us think about the idea of judgment day." —*Roy, Lowell, Vermont*

Lesson 4: Refiner's Fire

4.1 Scripture: Malachi 3:1-6

¹ "See, I am going to send My messenger, and he will clear the way before Me. Then the Lord you seek will suddenly come to His temple, the Messenger of the covenant you desire—see, He is coming," says the LORD of Hosts. ² But who can endure the day of His coming? And who will be able to stand when He appears? For He will be like a refiner's fire and like cleansing lye. ³ He will be like a refiner and purifier of silver; He will purify the sons of Levi and refine them like gold and silver. Then they will present offerings to the LORD in righteousness. ⁴ And the offerings of Judah and Jerusalem will please the LORD as in days of old and years gone by. ⁵ "I will come to you in judgment, and I will be ready to witness against sorcerers and adulterers; against those who swear falsely; against those who oppress the widow and the fatherless, and cheat the wage earner; and against those who deny justice to the foreigner. They do not fear Me," says the

LORD of Hosts. ⁶ *"Because I, Yahweh, have not changed, you descendants of Jacob have not been destroyed."*

4.2 Lesson Points

- 4.3.1. A messenger will come with an important announcement.
- 4.3.2. The One who follows the messenger is like a "refiner's fire."
- 4.3.3. The refining process makes Christians more acceptable servants to God.
- 4.3.4. The refining process heals the past.
- 4.3.5. The refining process leads to repentance of sin.
- 4.3.6. God provides countless opportunities for us to turn to Him.

4.3 Today's Lesson

4.3.1. A messenger will come with an important announcement.

Verse 1 - I am going to send My messenger, and he will clear the way before Me. Then the Lord you seek will suddenly come to His temple, the Messenger of the covenant you desire—see, He is coming!

- This is a prophetic reference to John the Baptist, who prepared the way for Jesus to come.
- It refers to the custom of the oriental kings in that time period to send a messenger ahead of them before the king would come for a visit.
- The messenger's job was two-fold:
- First, he was to remove any obstacles to the king's coming.

- Second, he was to make sure they planned an adequate reception for the king when he arrived.
- What obstacles keep people from accepting Jesus as Savior?

_____
_____
_____
_____
_____

- What obstacles keep Jesus from being fully Lord and Master of our lives or being ready for His return?

_____
_____
_____
_____
_____

- What kind of reception would Jesus receive if He came to our homes today?

_____
_____
_____
_____
_____

- What kind of reception would Jesus receive if He visited our church today?

_____
_____
_____
_____
_____

- What kind of reception would Jesus receive if He walked down the Main Street of our community today?

_____
_____
_____
_____

4.3.2. The One who follows the messenger is like a "refiner's fire."

Verse 2 - But who can endure the day of His coming? And who will be able to stand when He appears? For He will be like a refiner's fire and like cleansing lye.

- The people of Malachi's day did not like the way God was running the world.
- They had accused God of not being just because God had allowed bad things to happen.
- They asked where God was during times of crisis. They doubted God was really there.
- Malachi reminds them that one day the Lord was going to come.
- When the Lord comes, He will set right all that is evil and wrong.
- Malachi then asks the rhetorical question, "Who will be able to stand on that day?"
- This is an important question to think through because we have all done wrong at some point in our lives.
- We often think it is others who will be judged, but we must realize that we too will be judged one day and our own weaknesses and faults will be dealt with.
- We may not like the Lord's coming as much as we think we will!

- When the Lord comes, it will be like a refiner's fire. Fire in any form sounds dreadful, but a refiner's fire was unique.
- Think about the various types of fires that exist in the natural world.
- A forest fire rages out of control and destroys without concern for anyone or anything.
- An incinerator completely consumes whatever is put in it until nothing is left but dust.
- A refiner's fire refines. It purifies. It melts down a bar of silver or gold, separating out the impurities that lower the value. A refiner's fire does not rage out of control or destroy what it touches. It is controlled by the refiner and has a clear purpose.
- After the process is complete, the silver or gold is more valuable because it is more pure.
- When we go through difficult times in our lives we often think God has abandoned us, but in reality God is purifying us and making us more valuable to the Kingdom.
- Trials produce patience and patience produces maturity and maturity produces hope.
- Read Romans 5:3-4 and summarize those verses below:

_____
_____
_____
_____
_____

- Read James 1:2-4 and summarize those verses below:

_____
_____
_____
_____
_____

4.3.3. The refining process makes Christians more acceptable servants to God.

Verse 3 - . . . He will purify the sons of Levi and refine them like gold and silver. Then they will present offerings to the LORD in righteousness.

- Notice that the Lord will begin the purification process with the sons of Levi.
- In the Old Testament, the sons of Levi were the priests and religious leaders of the community.
- In the New Testament, each born-again Christian is a priest before God.
- Though this was referring to priests in Malachi's day, since we now live in the New Testament era, it refers to all born again Christians.
- When Christians are more pure in their faith, they are more useful to the Lord and to the community.

4.3.4. The refining process heals the past.

Verse 4 - And the offerings of Judah and Jerusalem will please the LORD as in days of old and years gone by.

- Once the purification process is over, then the offerings that people give to the Lord will please Him.
- The offerings will no longer be empty and meaningless because they will be given with a pure heart.
- Take a moment and reflect on these questions:
    - Do we offer our time, talent and treasure to God with a pure heart?
    - Or are we only looking for what we will get out of God?
- Malachi refers to the "days of old."

- We often refer to the past as the "good old days."
- One of the reasons they seem so good is that we tend to forget the bad parts and only remember the good parts.
- When we have been purified by fire, the Lord helps us heal from the past and look back on it with joy.

4.3.5. The refining process leads to repentance of sin.

Verse 5 - I will come to you in judgment . . .

- Judgment is often viewed as a negative thing in our society.
- But God's judgment is always correct because He knows the whole story.
- God is not fooled by fast talking lawyers or legal loopholes. God knows the truth and when He judges, He takes it all into account.
- Judgment can be a good thing if we have done what is right.
- That is why we must confess our sins to God and receive His forgiveness, so that we can be right with God when judgment comes.
- Read 1 John 1:9 and summarize it below:

  _____
  _____
  _____
  _____
  _____

- If we have sincerely confessed our sins and repented of those sins, then we will not be judged for them. They are gone forever!

- How does that truth make us feel?

4.3.6. God provides countless opportunities for us to turn to Him.

Verse 6 - "Because I, Yahweh, have not changed, you descendants of Jacob have not been destroyed.

- Malachi pointed out to the people that the only reason God had not destroyed them for their sin already was because God had not changed His promises to them.
- God had promised to be with the people and help them. Even though the people had broken their own promises, God had kept His.
- Thank God He is faithful to us when we are not faithful to Him.
- God is the God of the second chance, and the third chance and the ten thousandth chance.
- But one day, we will have our LAST chance and then all that will be left is judgment.
- If God is giving us a chance to turn from our sin right now and start doing right, we should not waste this chance because we never know which will be our last chance.

4.4 What Have We Learned?

- God sends people into our lives to warn us that He wants us to prepare to meet Him.

- God purifies His people through the fires of difficulty, but in the end, we are better people because of it.
- When we finally meet God, we will not be able to offer any excuses because God knows the truth.
- Therefore we should repent of our sin now and seek God's forgiveness while we have the chance.
- Some of us still need to take that first step in having a relationship with God and His Son, Jesus. Start by turning to page 83 to the section "Finding Real Hope" and consider praying to receive Christ!

4.5 We Are Listening!

Some of the responses we have received to this lesson include:

- "This refiner's fire concept helps. It takes the focus away from thinking, 'Why is God letting me suffer?' Christ and the apostles suffered many wrongs. Bad stuff happens in the world, so I see how God uses those moments to refine us." —*Darryl, S. Burlington, VT*
- "I have been through many troubles in my life. Now I see how God used those troubles to make me a better person." —*Joyce, Barre, VT*

Lesson 5: The Importance of Tithing

5.1 Scripture: Malachi 3:7-12

⁷ *"Since the days of your fathers, you have turned from My statutes; you have not kept them. Return to Me, and I will return to you," says the LORD of Hosts. But you ask: "How can we return?"* ⁸ *"Will a man rob God? Yet you are robbing Me!" You ask: "How do we rob You?" "By not making the payments of 10 percent and the contributions.* ⁹ *You are suffering under a curse, yet you —the whole nation—are still robbing Me.* ¹⁰ *Bring the full 10 percent into the storehouse so that there may be food in My house. Test Me in this way," says the LORD of Hosts. "See if I will not open the floodgates of heaven and pour out a blessing for you without measure.* ¹¹ *I will rebuke the devourer for you, so that it will not ruin the produce of your ground, and your vine in your field will not be barren," says the LORD of Hosts.* ¹² *"Then all the nations will consider you fortunate, for you will be a delightful land," says the LORD of Hosts.*

5.2 Lesson Points

- 5.3.1. We should return to God.
- 5.3.2. Do not rob God.
- 5.3.3. Let us give with the right attitude.
- 5.3.4. Let us give to escape the curse.
- 5.3.5. Giving changes our self-focus to a God-focus.
- 5.3.6. When we give 10 percent we will experience God's heavenly blessings.
- 5.3.7. When we are wise stewards we will experience God's temporal blessings.

5.3 Today's Lesson

5.3.1. We should return to God.

Verse 7 - Since the days of your fathers, you have turned from My statutes; you have not kept them. Return to Me, and I will return to you, says the LORD of Hosts.

- The Jews had been chosen by God as His special people.
- God desires to be their loving Father and to have a healthy fatherly relationship with them.
- But for most of their history, the Jews have struggled with letting God be their father.
- The Jews often worshipped idols.
- The Jews often failed to obey the commands that the Lord gave them, which were for their own protection and blessing.
- The Jews often went through the motions of religious rituals without thought for the meaning of those rituals.
- Sadly, many Jews are still living without God.

- Though we may not be ethnically Jewish, when we became Christians we were grafted into the promises of God and became His children.
- God desires to be our Father and to have a wonderful fatherly relationship with us.
- Regretfully, like the Jews, we also often run from God and fail to allow Him to be the Father we need.
- We need the same thing the Jews needed in Malachi's day, we need to return to God!
- When we finally quit trying to force things to work —which God has already said will not be helpful to us—it is a good time to return to God.
- In fact, anytime we realize that our way is not working, that is the right time to return to God.

5.3.2. Do not rob God.

Verse 8 - "Will a man rob God? Yet you are robbing Me!" You ask: "How do we rob You?" "By not making the payments of 10 percent and the contributions."

- When the Jews asked why God did not think they were really following Him, He brought up the subject of tithing.
- Tithing means giving 10% of our income back to the Lord.
- Tithing is an area that many Christians struggle with.
- The Bible mentions tithing at least 37 times.
- The Jews understood what a tithe was, they just seldom gave the tithe as consistently as they should have.
- God said that when we withhold our tithe from the Lord, we are robbing Him.
- We cannot have a good relationship with our Heavenly Father if we are robbing Him on a regular basis.

- Many people try to argue that tithing was ONLY an Old Testament principle and that it does not apply to the New Testament. But the New Testament also teaches tithing.

5.3.3. Let us give with the right attitude.

Matthew 23:23 - "Woe to you, scribes and Pharisees, hypocrites! You pay a tenth of mint, dill and cumin, yet you have neglected the more important matters of the law—justice, mercy, and faith. These things should have been done without neglecting the others."

- In this verse Jesus endorsed the tithe, but Jesus also made it clear that the attitude of our hearts is as important as our tithe.
- The Pharisees were great tithers, but failed to show justice, mercy, faithfulness and love to others.
- Jesus said they needed to tithe as well as show justice, mercy, faithfulness and love to others.
- What attitudes should we have when we give? Read each passage and find a key word that identifies these attitudes:
    - 2 Corinthians 9:7: _____
    - 1 John 3:17-18: _____
    - 1 Corinthians 4:2, 16:2: _____
    - 2 Corinthians 9:6, Luke 6:38: _____
    - Mark 12:43-44: _____
- With these attitudes we can better follow Christ's command to love our neighbors (Matthew 22:39).

5.3.4. Let us give to escape the curse.

Verse 9 - You are suffering under a curse, yet you . . . are still robbing Me.

- When we fail to tithe we step out from under the blessing of God.
- We live in a sin-cursed world. If we are not under God's blessing, then we are vulnerable to all the destruction that comes from the curse of sin that rests on the world.
- We often work as hard as we can to overcome financial problems and still feel like we are cursed. When we feel like that, we should consider what the prophet Haggai said.

5.3.5. Giving changes our self-focus to a God-focus.

Haggai 1:5-6 - Now, the LORD of Hosts says this: "Think carefully about your ways: You have planted much but harvested little. You eat but never have enough to be satisfied. You drink but never have enough to become drunk. You put on clothes but never have enough to get warm. The wage earner puts his wages into a bag with a hole in it."

- Haggai and Malachi were both saying the same thing about giving.
- There were times they had worked hard but saw no improvement in their financial situation.
- We experience this sometimes in our own lives and that is when we feel cursed.
- Haggai points out that this concept of blessing and cursing applies to other areas of life too.
- Some people never seem to find a sense of satisfaction in their job, family, marriage, accomplishments, or in anything else.
- People feel this way when they have not made God the priority in their lives.
- When God is not a priority in life, then life will not satisfy us no matter how hard we work to make it better. We will feel like we are cursed in every area of life.

- We can break free of the curse of self-focus and regain a God-focus in our lives.

5.3.6. When we give 10 percent we will experience God's heavenly blessings.

Verse 10 - "Bring the full 10 percent into the storehouse so that there may be food in My house. Test Me in this way," says the LORD of Hosts. "See if I will not open the floodgates of heaven and pour out a blessing for you without measure."

- We often are more driven by money than we realize. Therefore, when we get to the place where we can give generously to the Lord with the right attitude, it is an indicator that something has changed inside of us.
- When people first learn about tithing, their response is often that they simply cannot afford it.
- God says to test Him in tithing and see what He does through it.
- Many people tithe a few times and when a gold brick does not drop into the backyard, they think God failed the test.
- Still others mistake a 1960s folk song for a hymn, where the singer asks the Lord for a Mercedes Benz, a color TV, and a night on the town. So exactly what *are* those blessings from heaven promised by God? The list is long, but here are a few:
    - Proverbs 16:16: _____

    - Proverbs 18:10: _____

    - Joel 2:28, Mark 13:10: A heavenly blessing might be a "dream" or ideas that accomplish the global proclamation of the Good News; faithful tithing enables that goal.

- But we must tithe with the right attitude and we must do it faithfully in order to be blessed.
- God has infinite resources. Yet He asks us to participate in supplying His storehouse because He knows that we need to give of ourselves in order to find meaning in our lives.
- What are some ministries our church accomplishes because of faithful giving?

_____
_____
_____
_____

5.3.7. When we are wise stewards we will experience God's temporal blessings.

Verse 11 - "I will rebuke the devourer for you, so that it will not ruin the produce of your ground, and your vine in your field will not be barren," says the LORD of Hosts.

- When God says that He will bless us for tithing, it does not always mean we will find extra money.
- Sometimes it means that God will keep things that we already have from breaking.
- Sometimes it means God will help us find ways to be more productive with the money we already have.
- Good stewardship is more than just tithing, it is also handling the other 90% well.
- Describe a time we experienced God's temporal blessing as a result of tithing.

_____
_____
_____
_____

- Look back at Lesson 2, section 2.3.4., regarding our example to our children, and breaking bad behavior patterns in our families. Consider:
    - Did our parents teach us to tithe? _____
    - Are we following our parents' example, good or bad? _____
    - If we have children and give them an allowance, do we teach them to tithe?
    _____

5.4 What Have We Learned?

- We tend to wander from God, so we must constantly return to Him.
- Because we love money so much, part of returning to God includes giving God our wallet – through tithing.
- When we begin to tithe, with the right attitude, it demonstrates that something has changed inside of us. It shows that God is now our priority.
- God will bless us for faithful tithing – or we can choose to live outside His blessing and experience the full force of this sin cursed world.

5.5 We Are Listening!

Some of the responses we have received to this lesson include:

- "I have tithed faithfully for five decades. Though I experienced more than my fair share of corporate layoffs, I tithed on my unemployment funds. God honored that commitment, and I experienced many pay raises, some as high as 21%. I have a high credit score, and the Lord has shown me that I don't have

to rack up a lot of credit-card debt to enjoy life. Most importantly, tithing changes the way I think about money!" —*Anonymous, Vermont*
- "Thank you for being bold enough to share this message. May we all learn to practice tithing again." —*Frank, Spanish Fort, Alabama*

Lesson 6: The Law of Sowing and Reaping

6.1 Scripture: Malachi 3:13-18

[13] "Your words against Me are harsh," says the LORD. Yet you ask: "What have we spoken against You?" [14] You have said: "It is useless to serve God. What have we gained by keeping His requirements and walking mournfully before the LORD of Hosts? [15] So now we consider the arrogant to be fortunate. Not only do those who commit wickedness prosper, they even test God and escape." [16] At that time those who feared the LORD spoke to one another. The LORD took notice and listened. So a book of remembrance was written before Him for those who feared Yahweh and had high regard for His name. [17] "They will be Mine," says the LORD of Hosts, "a special possession on the day I am preparing. I will have compassion on them as a man has compassion on his son who serves him. [18] So you will again see the difference between the righteous and the

wicked, between one who serves God and one who does not serve Him."

6.2 Lesson Points

- 6.3.1. Are we complaining about God?
- 6.3.2. Are we questioning God's blessings?
- 6.3.3. Do we measure God by worldly standards?
- 6.3.4. Do we fellowship with other Christians?
- 6.3.5. Is our service worthy of God's books?
- 6.3.6. Do we give up our faith in troubled times?
- 6.3.7. Are we sowing good seed for a future harvest?

6.3 Today's Lesson

6.3.1. Are we complaining about God?

Verse 13 – "Your words against Me are harsh," says the LORD. Yet you ask: "What have we spoken against You?"

- The people in Malachi's day claimed to be followers of God yet they often disliked how God ran the universe. They frequently complained about how God worked.
- Most of us can relate to this better than we would like to admit because if we were honest we would have to admit that we do not always like how God runs things either.
- God heard their complaints and had Malachi confront them.
- The people quickly backpedaled and tried to pretend that they had not complained about God's activities.
- We often do this in our own lives. We complain about what God is doing, but when someone points it

out, we pretend that we feel a different way than we really do.

6.3.2. Are we questioning God's blessings?

Verse 14 - You have said: "It is useless to serve God. What have we gained by keeping His requirements and walking mournfully before the LORD of Hosts?"

- One of the specific complaints the people had was that it seemed to be useless to serve the Lord.
- They wanted to know what they were going to get out of serving God.
- Many of us wonder the same thing.
- The very question reveals something wrong at the heart level.
- Being a Christian is not about "getting," it is about giving.
- Jesus set the example when He left the glory of Heaven, came to earth and offered His life for us on the cross of Calvary.
- One of the reasons we sometimes question if our faith is doing enough for us is that we think it is all about us. But life is NOT all about us. It is about praising God while serving others.

6.3.3. Do we measure God by worldly standards?

Verse 15 - So now we consider the arrogant to be fortunate. Not only do those who commit wickedness prosper, they even test God and escape.

- The people in Malachi's day said that those who did wrong seemed to prosper more than those who did right.
- It also seemed that bad people tested God all the time and got away with it.
- Sometimes we feel this way about our own culture.

6.3.4. Do we fellowship with other Christians?

Verse 16 - At that time those who feared the LORD spoke to one another.

- Though it seemed like evil was winning, there was still a group who feared the Lord.
- That handful of people got together and "spoke" to one another.
- Like Malachi's time, it seems that evil is winning in our culture. This is why it is so important for God's people to get together and encourage each other.
- Instead of running right to our cars after church, we should stay around and talk to each other.
- We should invite people from church over to dinner in our homes or meet for lunch somewhere in town.
- We should be looking for ways to spend time together and encourage each other.

6.3.5. Is our service worthy of God's books?

Verse 16 - . . . The LORD took notice and listened. So a book of remembrance was written before Him for those who feared Yahweh and had high regard for His name.

- The Lord noticed those who still believed in Him and had banded together as a group to encourage and support each other.
- Not only did the Lord notice, but He created a book of remembrance to write their story.
- It was common in that time period for kings to keep various books of remembrance about special events or activities of special groups of people so that the people would not forget the experiences.
- These books were kept in the King's archives.
- God is the ultimate King of the universe.

- God has a number of books in His own heavenly library.
- Revelation 20:12 and Luke 10:20 say that God has a "book of life" in heaven in which the names of all believers are listed.
- Psalm 56:8 says that God has a "book of tears" which records the wanderings of David before he became the King of Israel.
- Psalm 139:16 says that God has a "book of births" which records what will happen in our lives before we are born.
- This verse in Malachi reveals that God also has a book of remembrance in heaven.
- This book contains the stories of how God's people encouraged each other when everyone else had abandoned faith in God.
- We should endeavor to encourage other Christians so God can rejoice as He writes our story in His book.

6.3.6. Do we give up our faith in troubled times?

Verse 17 - "They will be Mine," says the LORD of Hosts, "a special possession on the day I am preparing. I will have compassion on them as a man has compassion on his son who serves him."

- The Lord says that believers who stood together and encouraged each other when everyone else fell away from faith would hold a special place in His heart.
- When we are persecuted for our faith and we hang in there and encourage each other, the God of the universe notices us.
- But God does not just notice. He has compassion on the persecuted like a father showing compassion for his children when they struggle.
- None of us are perfect, but if we stand together in tough times, we can expect special grace from God who sees our struggles and has compassion on us.

- When we go through hard times, we need all the help and compassion from God that we can get.
- Times of trouble are the times we need to press in closer to the Lord and to other Christians, not to fall away from the Lord.

6.3.7. Are we sowing good seed for a future harvest?

Verse 18 - So you will again see the difference between the righteous and the wicked, between one who serves God and one who does not serve Him.

- God says that though it appears that evil is winning, He is keeping track of everything in His book of remembrance.
- One day that book will be brought out and read. On that day those who have followed the Lord and encouraged each other will be honored.
- Remember this important biblical truth: We reap what we sow.
- Read Galatians 6:7-8 and summarize it below:

_____
_____
_____
_____
_____

- Read Proverbs 22:8 and summarize it below:

_____
_____
_____
_____
_____

- Read Hosea 8:7 and summarize it below:

  _____
  _____
  _____
  _____

- Read Jeremiah 12:13 and summarize it below:

  _____
  _____
  _____
  _____

- Read Hosea 10:12 and summarize it below:

  _____
  _____
  _____
  _____

- Read Psalm 126:5 and summarize it below:

  _____
  _____
  _____
  _____

- People may think they have God fooled, but God is keeping track.
- Payday will come some day!
- The law of sowing and reaping is something that we cannot avoid.
- Sometimes we go through hard times because we are reaping the junk that we sowed a long time ago.
- But if we start sowing good stuff now, then eventually we will reap the blessings that sprout from the good seeds we are now sowing.

6.4 What Have We Learned?

- Life is sometimes hard and even Christians can get discouraged.
- When Christians get discouraged, it is easy to think that our faith is not helping us much and we can become envious of those who do not follow God.
- Instead of being envious, we must continue to cling to our faith and draw strength from fellow believers.
- When we do this, God notices and has special compassion on us in our difficulties.
- We reap what we sow and even if we are currently reaping difficulties because of past mistakes, if we start sowing righteousness, we will eventually reap the good that comes from that.

6.5 We Are Listening!

Some of the responses we have received to this lesson include:

- "Your first point on complaining about how God works reminds me of Paul's remedy, to 'Give thanks in everything, for this is God's will for you in Christ Jesus' (I Thes. 5:18, HCSB). Growing up, Mom would tell us that God wouldn't be happy if after saying grace, we began to complain about the food she put on the table!" —*Wayne, S. Burlington, VT*
- "I did not come to Christ until I was middle aged. By then, I had sown more than my share of wild oats. I am still reaping some of the bad weeds from my past. But as I have started to sow good seed, things are getting better." —*Chris, Barre, VT*

Lesson 7: Judgment Day

7.1 Scripture: Malachi 4

¹ "Surely the day is coming; it will burn like a furnace. All the arrogant and every evildoer will be stubble, and the day that is coming will set them on fire," says the LORD Almighty. "Not a root or a branch will be left to them. ² But for you who revere my name, the sun of righteousness will rise with healing in His wings. And you will go out and frolic like well-fed calves. ³ Then you will trample on the wicked; they will be ashes under the soles of your feet on the day when I act," says the LORD Almighty. ⁴ "Remember the law of my servant Moses, the decrees and laws I gave him at Horeb for all Israel. ⁵ "See, I will send the prophet Elijah to you before that great and dreadful day of the LORD comes. ⁶ He will turn the hearts of the parents to their children, and the hearts of the children to their parents; or else I will come and strike the land with total destruction."

7.2 Lesson Points

- 7.3.1. The day of Christ is at hand.
- 7.3.2. Jesus is the light and the hope of the world.
- 7.3.3. We must go and tell others of our hope in Jesus!

7.3 Today's Lesson

7.3.1. The day of Christ is at hand.

Verse 1 - Surely the day is coming . . . All the arrogant and every evildoer will be stubble, and the day that is coming will set them on fire . . .

- Chapter 3 began with refiner's fire, which purifies us but does not destroy us. This reminds us that God wants to use the difficult things in our lives to make us better people, not to destroy us.
- Chapter 3 ends with the warning that one day we will all reap what we have sown and the difference between the righteous and the wicked will be made clear. We accept this as just and right.
- Chapter 4 opens with a description of what happens when that day of judgment finally comes.
- Most of us do not like to think about judgment day, but avoiding the topic will not make it go away. Judgment day will happen eventually.
- The first time Jesus came, He came as a baby in manger. His message was one of grace and forgiveness.
- The next time Jesus comes, He will come as a judge. His message will be one of judgment and justice based on how we responded to the message He gave when He came the first time.

- For those who have followed Jesus faithfully, judgment is nothing to be afraid of.
- For those who have not followed Him, fear is an appropriate response!
- Obviously people want to know when judgment day will happen.
- Only God the Father knows exactly when that day will come.
- Read Matthew 24:35-36 and summarize it below:

_____
_____
_____
_____
_____

- God is keeping the date of judgment day a secret so that we cannot live like the Devil our entire lives and then try to get right the day before Jesus returns.
- Since that day is a secret, we do not need to invest countless hours trying to figure out when it will be.
- Read 1 Thessalonians 5:1-2 and summarize it below:

_____
_____
_____
_____
_____

- Thieves come when we least expect it. Likewise, judgment day will come as a surprise.
- God is delaying judgment day so that everyone in the world will have a chance to hear the Gospel and respond.

- Read 2 Peter 3:9-11 and summarize it below:

_____
_____
_____
_____
_____

- Though God's timing is not our timing, God is also not willing that any of His chosen ones should perish. Therefore, God is waiting for the last person who is going to believe to have the same chance as the first person who believed. Then the end will come, and it will not be pretty.
- Since we do not know when the end will be, our focus must be on living holy lives right now so that when Jesus returns, He will find us living rightly.
- Though we do not know when the end will come, we do know that the Gospel must be preached to every corner of the world before the end comes.
- Read Matthew 24:14 and summarize it below:

_____
_____
_____
_____
_____

- According to the "Joshua Project" there are 6,918 people groups around the world that still have no access to the Gospel.
- While that may sound like a lot, there were more than 10,000 groups with no access to the Gospel only a few years ago.
- God's Spirit is moving quickly to call His people to Himself.

- One day very soon we will see the fulfillment of Revelation 7:9-10. Read those verses and summarize them below:

  _____
  _____
  _____
  _____

- We also know that before judgment day happens the Lord will come back and gather up all His followers and take us to heaven.
- Read 1 Thessalonians 4:16-17 and summarize it below:

  _____
  _____
  _____
  _____

- When Christ returns Christians will be changed and all our imperfections will finally be removed in an instant.
- Read 1 Corinthians 15:51-53 and summarize it below:

  _____
  _____
  _____
  _____

- When Jesus returns we will all give an account of ourselves and our relationship with Jesus.

- Read Romans 14:10-12 and summarize it below:

  _____
  _____
  _____
  _____

- Those who had a relationship with Jesus will enter into the eternal reward of heaven.
- Read Matthew 25:31-34 and summarize it below:

  _____
  _____
  _____
  _____

- Those who did not have a relationship with Jesus will have no place left to go but to the eternal punishment of hell.
- Read Matthew 25:41, 46 and summarize it below:

  _____
  _____
  _____
  _____

- Note that hell was never designed for people. Hell was designed for the Devil and his demons. But for those who reject Jesus, there is no other place for them to spend eternity, so they go to hell.

7.3.2. Jesus is the light and the hope of the world.

Verse 2 - But for you who revere my name, the sun of righteousness will rise with healing in His wings. And you will go out and frolic like well-fed calves.

- Jesus is the sun of righteousness because He is the Light of the world and the only person who was ever completely righteous.
- Those of us who have discovered a relationship with Jesus will not experience eternal judgment. Instead we will finally experience healing from the sun of righteousness!
- Notice the phrase "healing in His wings." In those days, Jews wore an outer garment called the *Tallit*. It was a shawl-like garment of wool or silk with fringes at the four corners. It was commonly referred to as a prayer shawl. The corners of the shawl were known as "wings."
- As a Jew, Jesus would have worn a *Tallit* regularly. Therefore, in a figurative sense, Jesus would have had "wings" because the edges hanging down from his prayer shawl would have been called that.
- Take a moment to read the story of the sick woman in Luke 8:42-48 who quietly came up behind Jesus and touched Him.
- This woman had been sick all of her life. She had spent all of her money going to doctors, but they had not been able to help her. She had heard about the healing power of Jesus and believed that if she could just touch the edge of His garment, she would be healed. She wove her way through the crowd and touched Him. She instantly experienced healing from the "wings" of the Sun of Righteousness.
- On judgment day all who follow Jesus will finally be healed of all their physical sicknesses.
- More importantly, on that day, all who follow Jesus will finally be healed of the sin sickness that has plagued us since our birth!
- That will make us free from the burdens that have held us back and we will be like young animals running around the fields playing and having fun.

- Hallelujah, what a Savior! We must do all that we can to ensure that we are ready for that day!

7.3.3. We must go and tell others of our hope in Jesus!

Verse 5 – See, I will send the prophet Elijah to you before that great and dreadful day of the LORD comes.

- One way to be ready for that day is to be watching for the prophet "Elijah" who will prepare us to receive Jesus when He comes.
- This prophecy was fulfilled literally 430 years later when John the Baptist came and proclaimed that Jesus was the Messiah and prepared the way for the Jews to receive Jesus.
- Though some people argue whether John the Baptist was the fulfillment of this prophecy or not, we know John the Baptist was the fulfillment of this prophecy because the angel Gabriel said he would be in Luke 1:11-17.
- Jesus also said John the Baptist was the fulfillment of that prophecy in Matthew 17:10-13.
- John the Baptist was the literal fulfillment of this prophecy; but in a practical sense, God is using people today as modern-day "Elijahs" to help others discover faith in Christ.
- We have had many "Elijahs" help us find faith.
- We should seek to be an Elijah to someone else.
- Make a list of people that God has been leading us to pray for and talk to about Christ. Have we invited them to church?

_____
_____
_____
_____

- These are the days of Elijah and we should be the voice of Elijah crying out!

7.4 What Have We Learned?

- God is gracious and gives us many chances, but when the end finally comes we had better be ready because all our chances will be used up.
- It is impossible to know when that end will be, so we should live holy lives ready for Jesus' return.
- When Jesus returns, it will be a great day of healing for those who followed Him but a terrible day of judgment for those who rejected Him.
- We must be an "Elijah" to help others find faith in Christ so they can be ready when Jesus returns.

7.5 We Are Listening!

Some of the responses we have received to this lesson include:

- "That day is coming. We must be ready. Even if Jesus' return is years away, any day could be our last day!" —*Ken, Phoenix, AZ*
- "This really helps me focus on living right instead of just having head knowledge about end times." —*Neal, Williamstown, VT*

Outline for Malachi

Malachi: Finding Hope in the Midst of Adversity............1

Introduction..5

Lesson 1: Tough Love..7
   1.1 Scripture: Malachi 1:1-3, 6-9, 14............................7
   1.2 Lesson Points...8
   1.3 Today's Lesson..8
      1.3.1. God speaks to man..8
      1.3.2. God loves man..9
      1.3.3. God deserves honor.......................................12
      1.3.4. God deserves our sacrifice.............................13
      1.3.5. God deserves our best....................................14
      1.3.6. Do we receive much and give little?...............15
      1.3.7. God is King among nations............................15
   1.4 What Have We Learned?.......................................16
   1.5 We Are Listening!..16

Lesson 2: A Covenant of Life and Peace...........................17
   2.1 Scripture: Malachi 2:1-9..17
   2.2 Lesson Points...18
   2.3 Today's Lesson..18
      2.3.1. Spiritual leaders should set an example.........18
      2.3.2. Christians should be an example to society...20
      2.3.3. Christians should not be a curse to others.....20
      2.3.4. Christian parents are an example to their children..21
      2.3.5. God promises life and peace..........................25
      2.3.6. Spiritual leaders must speak the truth............25
      2.3.7. Spiritual leaders guard the knowledge of God.
....26

  2.3.8. Christians should not be the cause of others turning away from God................................26
  2.3.9. The shame of sin should lead to repentance. 27
 2.4 *What Have We Learned?*......................................27
 2.5 *We Are Listening!*..28

Lesson 3: Have We Wearied the Lord?.........................29
 3.1 Scripture: Malachi 2:10-17...................................29
 3.2 Lesson Points...30
 3.3 Today's Lesson..30
  3.3.1. Christians should not deal treacherously with each other..30
  3.3.2. Christians should only marry fellow believers. 31
  3.3.3. Christians should turn away from sin............33
  3.3.4. Christians should not lust after another spouse. 33
  3.3.5. Christians should produce spiritual fruit........34
  3.3.6. Christians should not weary God with insincerity...35
 3.4 What Have We Learned?....................................37
 3.5 We Are Listening!..38

Lesson 4: Refiner's Fire..39
 4.1 Scripture: Malachi 3:1-6......................................39
 4.2 Lesson Points...40
 4.3 Today's Lesson..40
  4.3.1. A messenger will come with an important announcement...40
  4.3.2. The One who follows the messenger is like a "refiner's fire."..42
  4.3.3. The refining process makes Christians more acceptable servants to God...................................44
  4.3.4. The refining process heals the past..............44
  4.3.5. The refining process leads to repentance of sin. 45
  4.3.6. God provides countless opportunities for us to turn to Him...46

    4.4 What Have We Learned?..46
    4.5 We Are Listening!...47
Lesson 5: The Importance of Tithing...................................49
    5.1 Scripture: Malachi 3:7-12...................................49
    5.2 Lesson Points...50
    5.3 Today's Lesson..50
        5.3.1. We should return to God................................50
        5.3.2. Do not rob God...51
        5.3.3. Let us give with the right attitude...................52
        5.3.4. Let us give to escape the curse.....................52
        5.3.5. Giving changes our self-focus to a God-focus.
....53
        5.3.6. When we give 10 percent we will experience God's heavenly blessings..54
        5.3.7. When we are wise stewards we will experience God's temporal blessings..55
    5.4 What Have We Learned?..56
    5.5 We Are Listening!...56
Lesson 6: The Law of Sowing and Reaping.........................59
    6.1 Scripture: Malachi 3:13-18...................................59
    6.2 Lesson Points...60
    6.3 Today's Lesson..60
        6.3.1. Are we complaining about God?....................60
        6.3.2. Are we questioning God's blessings?............61
        6.3.3. Do we measure God by worldly standards?...61
        6.3.4. Do we fellowship with other Christians?.........62
        6.3.5. Is our service worthy of God's books?...........62
        6.3.6. Do we give up our faith in troubled times?.....63
        6.3.7. Are we sowing good seed for a future harvest?
....64
    6.4 What Have We Learned?..66
    6.5 We Are Listening!...66
Lesson 7: Judgment Day..67
    7.1 Scripture: Malachi 4..67
    7.2 Lesson Points...68

7.3 Today's Lesson..68
    7.3.1. The day of Christ is at hand...........................68
    7.3.2. Jesus is the light and the hope of the world.. .72
    7.3.3. We must go and tell others of our hope in Jesus!...74
7.4 What Have We Learned?..75
7.5 We Are Listening!...75

About the Author

Dr. Terry W. Dorsett has served on the pastoral staff of one of America's largest congregations, Thomas Road Baptist Church in Lynchburg, Virginia, where he learned key concepts about reaching a region for Christ. He has also served as the pastor of small churches in Vermont, the least churched state in America. Since 2001 Dr. Dorsett has served as the Director of Missions for the Green Mountain Baptist Association. In that role he helps start new churches and plans strategic evangelism projects for existing churches. Having served both large and small churches, in both city and rural areas, he has a unique perspective on healthy church growth. Learn more about this ministry at www.vermontbaptist.org.

Terry has written numerous articles on church growth, bivocational ministry and postmodern evangelism. He is a frequent contributor to Baptist Press. Terry's blog, www.terrydorsett.com, is read by over 1,500 people a month. He is the author of four previous books: *Developing Leadership Teams in the Bivocational Church*, *Bible Brain Teasers: Fun Adventures through the Bible*, *Creating Effective Partnerships - Strategies for Increasing Kingdom Impact*, and *Mission Possible: Reaching the Next Generation Through the Small Church*.

Terry holds a Bachelors Degree in Interdisciplinary Studies from Liberty University, a Masters of Religious Education from Liberty Baptist Theological Seminary, and a Doctor of Ministry in Mission Administration from Golden Gate Baptist Theological Seminary.

Also from Dr. Terry W. Dorsett

	Developing Leadership Teams in the Bivocational Church Written by a small-church bivocational pastor, this book includes lessons for building teams who will work alongside their pastor to share in ministry. CrossBooks, Division of LifeWay, 2010 ISBN: 978-1-6150-7252-1 Available at: crossbooks.com, amazon.com, barnesandnoble.com
	Bible Brain Teasers: Fun Adventures Through the Bible This collection of more than 70 Bible puzzles and activities will engage young people in learning the Bible in fun ways. Even adults will enjoy testing their Bible knowledge. Lulu Enterprises, Inc., 2011 ISBN: 978-1-257-78532-2 Available at: amazon.com, lulu.com, barnesandnoble.com
	Creating Effective Partnerships - Strategies for Increasing Kingdom Impact Use this Leader's Guide and Student Workbook for seminars on building ministry partnerships. Lulu Enterprises, Inc., 2012 ISBN: 978-1-105-08483-6 Available at: amazon.com, lulu.com
	**Mission Possible: Reaching the Next Generation through the Small Church** By understanding how the next generation thinks, church leaders will be able to more effectively communicate the timeless truths of scripture to a new generation. CrossBooks, Division of LifeWay, 2012 ISBN: 978-1-462-71379-0 Available at: crossbooks.com, amazon.com, barnesandnoble.com

Finding Real Hope

We all face adversity in our lives. Though the world offers many ways to face adversity, the world's methods fail when adversity intensifies. But God offers hope to us through His Son Jesus Christ. When we place our hope in Christ alone, we find new purpose for living, new strength to endure, new hope in times of adversity, and a hope that never fails. To find new hope in Christ, consider praying a prayer like this:

- Lord, thank You for loving me and dying on the cross for me. I now turn from my own way of living and place all my hope and faith in You. Forgive me of my many sins and help me to serve You faithfully for the rest of my life. Amen.

If you prayed this prayer, tell a friend about it. Contact Dr. Terry Dorsett through his website, www.terrydorsett.com, and let him know what God is doing in your life.